Heidegger's Lizard

Alice Brière-Haquet

Stencil illustrations by Sophie Vissière

INTRODUCTION

In this story, Heidegger is exploring the relationship between "beings" and the world. In what way does each – the rock, the lizard and the human – relate to the world around them? For Heidegger, there are ways of belonging to the world. While the rock is merely part of the world, the lizard inhabits the world but without quite grasping the world. The human, however, genuinely dwells in the world and relates to it as such – which, Heidegger argues, sets us apart from non-human animals.

Martin Heidegger (1889–1976) is one of the most influential – and controversial – philosophers of the twentieth century. He is often associated with existentialism and phenomenology, and his work was enormously influential. However, his reputation is marred by his association with, and support for, the Nazi Party in Germany. His lack of a repudiation later in life proved frustrating for many.

There is a stone and
there is the Sun.

The Sun heats the stone,
but the stone does not know it.

It's just there.

There is a lizard
passing through.

He crosses the grass
in search of a stone and
its warmth.

And he stays there for hours.
Content to be there.

But there is a lot he does not know.

He does not know that the
stone is called stone.

He does not even know that
its warmth comes from the Sun.

He knows nothing of the
Sun and the planets,
and all those that
revolve in the universe.

A child comes along;
his name is Pierre.

He runs in the warmth
of the Sun and dances
with the movement
of the planets.

This child scares
the lizard...

...who leaves,
looking for another stone.

A stone he thinks is the Sun.